THE ULTIMATE GUIDE TO DISCIPLINING WITHOUT DAMAGE : Guide on how to get your kid behave without damage.

Antonio Lawrence

TABLE OF CONTENTS

Chapter 1

chapter 2

Chapter 3

Chapter 4

Chapter 5

Chapter 1

What discipline is and not

Punishment and discipline have quite different purposes when it comes to dealing with your child's misbehaving. While discipline aims to teach a child how to make a better decision next time, punishment concentrates on making a child suffer for disobeying the rules.

What Is Penalty?
Punishment imposes a cost for a child's transgression. Making a child "pay" for his errors is the goal. Sometimes a parent's frustration leads them to want to punish their child. Sometimes it comes from a place of desperation. To make it clear to a child that his behavior must improve "or else," a parent may feel compelled to yell at him, spank him, or take away every privilege he has ever enjoyed.

Instead of teaching a child to exercise self-control, punishment aims to control them. Additionally, punishment frequently modifies a child's self-concept.

If a child receives severe discipline, they may start to believe that they are bad. He might think he's a bad person instead of thinking he made a bad decision. Kids are most likely to receive discipline from authoritative parents.

1. Physical pain and suffering are intended effects of punishment, such as spanking. Other examples of punishment could be calling a child names or making a teenager hold a sign that reads, "I steal from stores."

Why Some Parents Have Problems With Punishing Their Children
Children don't learn good behavior through punishment.

2. A young child who is spanked for hitting his brother does not learn how to settle disputes amicably. Instead, he'll be perplexed as to why hitting his brother is prohibited but hitting you is acceptable. Children who get punishment learn that they are powerless over themselves. They discover they cannot control their behavior on their own and that their parents must do so.

Children who get harsh punishment may focus more on their resentment against the person who caused them harm than on the root of their misbehavior.

A child who is made to sit in the corner for hours can therefore choose to think about ways to exact revenge on the caregiver instead of sitting and considering how he can perform better the next time.

Discipline: What Is It?

Children learn new skills through discipline, including how to control their conduct, work through issues, and handle uncomfortable emotions. Children that are disciplined are taught socially acceptable ways to deal with negative emotions like anger and disappointment as well as how to learn from their mistakes. Techniques for enforcing discipline can be time-outs or the denial of privileges.

3. The objective is to provide children with a definite adverse consequence that will enable them to make wiser decisions in the future.

Discipline employs a strict method. Giving children clear norms and applying consistent punitive measures when they violate them constitutes healthy discipline. 4 The timing of consequences is also important. So while a parent may punish a child by taking away all devices permanently, a parent may discipline a child by taking away the TV for 24 hours if they won't turn it off.

Both favorable and unfavorable effects
Advantages of Discipline
Instead of being reactive, discipline is proactive. Numerous behavioral issues are

avoided, and it guarantees that kids are actively learning from their mistakes. 5 Positive tactics, such compliments and reward schemes, are used in many disciplinary techniques. Children are given obvious incentives to follow the rules when they get positive reinforcement, which promotes excellent conduct to persist.

Positive ties between parents and children are also fostered by discipline. And often frequently, that positive connection lowers attention-seeking behavior and encourages kids to act appropriately. Discipline is not about humiliating children, even when it allows for appropriate amounts of guilt. And it's important that. Children who are confident in themselves are less prone to make bad decisions. He will instead have faith in his capacity to control his conduct.

chapter 2

Positive discipline

Why positive discipline?
"Parents don't want to yell or hurt their kids. We do it because we're overwhelmed and don't see another way," explains Professor Cluver.

The data is clear: yelling and beating simply do not work and may cause more damage than good in the long run. Repeated yelling and striking might potentially severely effect a child's whole life. The prolonged "toxic stress" it causes may lead to a number of undesirable effects including greater odds of school dropout, depression, drug use, suicide and heart disease.

"It's like saying: here's this medication, it's not going to help you and it's going to make you sick," adds Professor Cluver. "When we know something doesn't work, that's a really solid reason to seek for a another approach."

Rather than punishment and what not to do, the positive discipline method places a focus on creating a good connection with your kid and setting expectations around conduct. The good news for every parent is it works and here's how you can start putting it into practice:

1. Plan 1-on-1 time
One-on-one time is vital for creating any healthy connection and much more so with your children. "It may be 20 minutes a day. Or even 5 minutes. You can mix it with things like washing dishes together as you sing a song or conversing while you're hanging out the clothes," adds Professor

Cluver. "What's very essential is that you concentrate on your kid. So, you put your TV off, you turn your phone off, you go to their level and it's you and them."

2. Praise the positives

As parents we frequently concentrate on our children's negative conduct and call it out. Children may see this as a means to obtain your attention, prolonging terrible behavior rather than putting a stop to it.

Children thrive on praise. It helps them feel appreciated and unique. "Watch out for when they're doing something positive and reward them, even if that thing is simply playing for five minutes with their sibling," suggests Professor Cluver. "This may promote excellent conduct and lessen the need for discipline."

3. Set clear expectations

"Telling your kid precisely what you want them to do is significantly more successful than telling them what not to do," says Professor Cluver. "When you ask a youngster to not create a mess, or to be kind, they don't necessarily grasp what they're expected to do." Clear directions like "Please pick up all of your toys and put them in the box" provide a clear expectation and enhance the probability that they'll accomplish what you're asking.

"But it's necessary to establish reasonable expectations. Asking them to keep quiet for a full day may not be as doable as asking for 10 minutes of quiet time while you take a phone call," says Professor Cluver. "You know what your kid is capable of. But if you ask for the impossible, they are going to fail."

4. Distract artistically

When your kid is being difficult, diverting them with a more pleasant activity might be a good tactic suggests Professor Cluver. "When you redirect them towards something else - by changing the subject, proposing a game, taking them into another room, or going for a stroll, you may effectively divert their energy into good behavior."

Timing is also key. Distraction is also about identifying when things are going to go awry and taking action. Being observant of when your kid is beginning to grow fidgety, irritated or upset, or when two siblings are eyeing the same object, may help alleviate a potential conflict before it becomes one.

5. Use calm consequences

Part of growing up is understanding that if you do something, something may happen as a consequence. Defining this for your kid is a simple procedure that fosters improved conduct while educating them about responsibility.

Give your kid a chance to do the right thing by explaining the repercussions of their poor conduct. As an example, if you want your kid to stop scribbling on the walls, you might urge them to stop or else you will terminate their play time. This offers them with a warning and a chance to adjust their behaviors.

If they don't stop, follow through with the penalties gently and without expressing irritation, "and give yourself credit for that — it's not easy!" adds Professor Cluver.

If they do stop, offer them heaps of praise for it, suggests Professor Cluver. "What you are doing is building a positive feedback loop for your kid. Calm consequences have been demonstrated to be helpful for youngsters to learn about what occurs when they act badly."

Being consistent is a critical aspect in excellent parenting, which is why following through with the consequences is essential. And so is making them believable. "You can take a teenager's phone away for an hour but taking it away for a week could be harder to follow through on."

Engaging with younger children

One-on-one time may be entertaining — and it's absolutely free! "You may replicate their emotions, smash spoons against pots, or sing together," says Professor Cluver. "There's fantastic evidence indicating that playing with your children increases their brain development."

Engaging with older children

Like younger children, teens desire praise and want to be thought of as good.

One-on-one time is still vital to them. "They enjoy it if you dance around the room with them or engage in a discussion about their favourite singer," adds Professor Cluver. "They may not always show it, but they do. And, it's an efficient approach of creating a connection on their terms."

While setting expectations, "ask children to help design some of the rules," recommends Professor Cluver. "Sit them down and attempt to agree on the home dos and don'ts. They may also assist determine what the repercussions for poor conduct will be.

Being active in the process lets them realize that you recognize they're becoming their own autonomous beings."

Chapter 3

Discipline but never punishment

When we speak about discipline, we generally refer to the attempts of parents and teachers to limit or eliminate bothersome or improper kid behaviors. Punishment is meant to inhibit or restrict behavior and may look like the ideal complement for these purposes. The word "discipline" incorporates the concepts of training but also of punishment.

From the viewpoint of psychological research, there is another method to examine the problem of discipline that sidesteps a pure emphasis on punishment. This method starts with what we are attempting to achieve - reducing improper kid behaviors and instilling habits and values. This approach preserves the same aims, but very much opens up the various ways of accomplishing these goals without the use of punishment.

Punishment in Brief

As a general rule, punishment is not a particularly successful technique of modifying behavior, at least in the ordinary manner it is applied. By punishment, I refer to negative consequences following particular conduct (e.g., mild rebuke, lecture, yelling, or beating) or eliminating some good result (e.g., putting the kid in time out or away from desired activities, taking away a privilege) (e.g., placing the child in time out or away from desirable events, taking away a privilege).

As an aside, gentle, rational, and measured reasoning with a child (e.g., "We do not do that [behavior] in this house," "What if your sister ruined your toys?" or "You, just violated a Kantian imperative") are wonderful to teach reasoning and to model parent reasonableness under fire but not very effective as behavior-change techniques.

There are three key considerations pertinent to the use of punishment.

1. Punishment even at its finest, does not produce the beneficial behavior the parents seek.

That is, it does not educate the youngster what to do, but may temporary inhibit the unwanted behavior. You may chastise the kid all day for not (pick one: completing schoolwork, playing a musical instrument, cleaning up her room) but it will not educate her to do homework, to practice, or to clean up. Developing behavior does not come from just repressing unpleasant actions.

2. Punishment typically has undesirable side effects

These impacts include seeking to flee from or avoid the event or person associated with punishment, emotional affects (e.g., weeping, being angry), and engaging in hostile conduct. None of the side effects corresponds to the efficiency of punishment (e.g., the more upset the kid is not any indicator of the success of punishment in suppressing conduct) (e.g., the more upset the child is not any indication of the effectiveness of punishment in suppressing behavior). Actually, adverse effects "come on" or occur even with relatively inadequate punishment.

3. The punishment trap might lock in punishment in parent and teacher conduct.

That trap relates to the fact that punishment frequently stops the activity promptly — sometimes by fright or interruption. These immediate impacts (halt of the adverse kid behavior) help lock in the parent's conduct (via negative reinforcement) (through negative reinforcement). By "locking in" I mean it enhances the possibility that the parent will punish in the future. In reality, the pace of the child's misbehavior is not modified or improved, but those delayed consequences do not overwhelm the benefit of instant suspension of conduct.

To be clear, disciplining your child's conduct may have numerous aims. For example, parents frequently wish to teach a lesson, offer an appropriate sentence to match the child's offense, to be a responsible or "good parent", or to follow cultural or religious norms. These aims may be distinct from modifying child behavior.

The aims may not always contradict, i.e., eradicating certain behavior, but the methods truly do. For example, when your kid accidentally breaks the family playhouse that was made by his or her great-great-great (keep adding "greats") grandpa from Pangaea, the supercontinent, you may wish to emphasize the severity of the act and punish appropriately. At this stage, a psychologist equipped with "evidence-based" punishment may readily remark, "the research supports usage of only a few minutes of time out or short loss of a privilege (e.g., internet, movies, bicycle) for a day." The psychologist is referring about behavior change but not the numerous objectives that you, as a parent, desire to attain.

So, How to Eliminate Behavior without Punishment

There is little evidence that punishment is truly required to meet parent objectives or to discipline children. That is a clear statement and arguing that it has a solid scientific background is no comfort.

Here is what we know. There are techniques of removing behavior that include explicitly generating and encouraging behaviors that are contrary to or incompatible with the behavior one wishes to eradicate.

The non-technical concept is reinforcing positive opposites. This is based on various technical approaches (multiple differential reinforcement schedules) that have been widely investigated in human and nonhuman animal research (see references) (see references). Essentially, the main element is creating the behavior one intends rather than concentrating on what to remove.

Where Does Punishment Fit in All of This?

The first point to highlight is that punishment is always the secondary component of any behavior-change endeavor when trying to "discipline." That means we begin by identifying the behavior we desire to take the place of the one we want to eradicate. We now concentrate on developing that behavior via the use of antecedents and consequences and shaping. Once that core focus is in place, moderate punishment may be a helpful supplement.

Here are crucial strategies for using punishment effectively:

1. Emphasize praise and attention on the good opposite behaviors.

If you are using a time out from reinforcement as the punishment, do not expect it to work at all unless you are praising the right conduct you desire during moments when your kid is not in time out.

2. If punishment is to be utilized, keep it gentle and short.

Time out of a few minutes (e.g., 5 minutes or roughly) or loss of privilege (e.g., for an evening or day or two) is as effective as what you would wish to do (e.g., 1 hour of time out; taking away the privilege of going out on dates till your kid is 30 years old) (e.g., 1 hour of time out; taking away the privilege of going out on dates until your child is 30 years old).

3. Explain to your youngster why he or she should or should not do anything.

It is OK and even advantageous to do so. This represents thinking, reasoning, and the right way of managing a potentially dangerous issue. Yet, it is not likely to alter the frequency of the improper activity. The common parental mantra, "If I have told you once, I have told you a thousand times" makes perfect sense. That expression is in accord with what we know, namely, advising someone to do something (e.g., quit smoking, eat more vegetables, lighten up on the fast foods, add broccoli to your diet) does not imply they will do it. Providing knowledge may assist but, done in isolation, it is not a highly dependable technique to influence behavior in most individuals most of the time.

4. Avoid physical punishment.

It is not more effective and, in fact, moderate to severe use raises the risk for all kinds of unpleasant consequences (e.g., aggressive and antisocial behavior, poor school performance, difficulties of physical health, harm to the immune system) (e.g., aggressive and antisocial behavior, poor school performance, problems of physical health, damage to the immune system). The uses of physical punishment are determined by hundreds of other elements, of course. And frequently the conclusions are not applicable to families or compete with what they have experienced (e.g., punishment trap is pertinent here) (e.g., punishment trap is relevant here).

5. Model the conduct you hope to see in your kid.

Modeling is an underutilized influence in the home, i.e., displaying precisely the behaviors you desire your kid to acquire. Children mimic parents of course, but modeling is rarely utilized strategically by parents to teach the behaviors they desire in a methodical fashion.

6. Avoid cliché interventions.

Our media has promoted approaches like "tough love," "three strikes (misbehaviors) and you are out," or reasoning that is not actually well established in childrearing research (e.g., slippery slope—if I let this go, my child will keep getting worse). These are not treatments that are helpful as a general rule, and they really may make accomplishing the targeted behaviors much more difficult..

Chapter 4

Teaching them without anger, shame or blame

What Is Shaming?
Wondering precisely what constitutes humiliating a child? Here are several examples:

Telling humiliating or revealing anecdotes in an effort to alter the child's attitude or conduct

Taking what should be a private dialogue about conduct and consequences and making it public by sharing it with friends, family, or the world at large (through social media) (via social media)

Intentionally making a youngster feel horrible about himself or herself, as a person, instead than concentrating on the actual behavior you're attempting to modify

Sadly, these approaches might appear to work in the beginning, but humiliating your kid will rapidly backfire. And although parents have undoubtedly used shame from the beginning of time, the accessibility of social media makes it more harmful than ever. Not only do you lose enormous relationship equity, but humiliating kids in public or online also rips down trust and self-esteem. At the same time, it zaps your child's drive to participate in the precise activities you're attempting to promote.

Guilt vs. Shame

What's puzzling for parents is that ideas and emotions actually impact behavior. For example, if you screamed at your kids and then felt a sense of remorse or regret, such sentiments could be enough to help you modify your behavior. But there's a distinction between guilt and shame.

Brené Brown, a research professor at the University of Houston and the author of the New York Times best-selling book "Daring

Greatly," explains the distinction between guilt and shame:

Guilt states "I did a horrible thing."
Shame says, "I am awful."
No of what behavioral difficulties you're dealing with right now, that's not a message you want to give to your kids.

Why Shaming Your Kids Doesn't Work
Shaming youngsters is especially problematic since shame tends to be a sensation that remains around, and it frequently lasts longer than you realize or want. So although it may appear on the surface that parents who humiliate their kids on social media receive results, know that this approach to parenting really undermines two things you're trying hard to create:

Your child's self-esteem
Your long-term partnership

For some, there may also be a relationship between the reach of public shaming and its long-term repercussions. For example, shaming your child publicly on Facebook, where there's a perception that a very large number of people are seeing it, may be more harmful to your relationship and your child's sense of self than the old-fashioned "You won't believe what he did now!" kind of shaming that used to take place around the dinner table in front of Aunt Sally.

What If You've Already Publicly Shamed Your Kids?
Let's get genuine. You could be reading this and thinking, "Oh no! I've previously done this." Now's your moment to apologize. Your kids need to know that you're human and prepared to admit your faults. So even if you're feeling a degree of sorrow that makes it exceedingly tough to begin the discussion, make it happen.

If you've publicly embarrassed your kid, he or she needs to hear you really apologize and express clearly assurance that it won't happen again.

A real apology will have a healing impact on your relationship so that you may begin to utilize your connection as your strongest 'weapon' for influencing your child's behavior—not shame.

Shaming Words Single Parents Should Avoid
Some single parents may be at more risk for turning to humiliating their kids because of the stress that typically surrounds interacting with your ex. Here's a list of embarrassing words and phrases you'll want to avoid:

"You're such a nasty girl." This allegation doesn't assist your kid comprehend what she's done wrong or what she needs to improve. And it's absolutely not a term you want rattling around in her mind for years to come!

"You're exactly like your mother (or father)." This may be every bit as embarrassing as the "you're a horrible girl" scenario, particularly if your kid knows you have a lot of hatred and strife with your ex.

"I don't know why I even bother with you." Imagine what that one feels like for a second. Most of the time, this one is utilized out of pure irritation. To prevent getting to that point in the first place, be deliberate about taking care of yourself and carving out some me-time when you need it.

"I should send you off to live with dad (or mum)" This is similar to the sentence above, and it not only shows frustration, but it also reduces your parental authority. You're essentially indicating that you're out of alternatives. And if you feel that way, pause and take a long breath. Then surround yourself with your support system and plan out your next moves. If your ex is participating, be careful to engage him or her in the talk, too, particularly if you fear your child's habits may be placing him at danger.

"I'm so weary of dealing with you." Stop this phrase at "I'm very exhausted." Period. And then take a break and get some rest. A new viewpoint can help you handle any challenges you're facing with your kid without hurting his self-esteem or your relationship.

How to Influence Your Kids' Behavior Without Shaming

The absolute greatest instrument you have at your disposal for influencing your kids' conduct is your connection. Ideally, you want to develop a link that promotes your kids' positive sense of who they are, while simultaneously providing them freedom to learn from their errors. So when your kids choose to defy you, have a talk about their choices and what they can do better next time. Here are some examples of positive words and phrases you may use:

"I'd want you to tell me what occurred." Take a few minutes to hear your youngster out before you answer.

"What did it feel like for you?" Help your youngster identify the emotions related with the events that had transpired. These may include wrath, fear, loneliness, astonishment, and others.

"What could you have done differently?" This is a huge one! Ideally, you want your kid to identify for himself or herself the options that may have been more beneficial.

At this point, it's crucial for you to confirm thoughts that may have been beneficial. The objective is to empower your kid with ideas for 'next time' rather than shame your child not picking those alternatives the first time around.

"What will you do next time?" Solidify the power of your child's statements by having him or her pick a top tactic.

"How can I help?" This one is typically left out, but it's incredibly strong! Even if there's nothing tangible you can do, it will assist your youngster to hear you make a sincere offer to aid

Utilizing of uplifting words rather than using words of criticism

Chapter 5

Praise in public correct in private

Be sincere with praise

If praise is to be at all effective, it must be authentic. Don't reward a youngster for being silent 10 seconds after he was yelling. Our youngsters see straight through fake praise. They realize it is pointless. The secret to complimenting in public is to get to them before they have the opportunity to misbehave.

Correct in private

If all of your efforts to praise your kid have little impact, do what you can to correct it in private. Be proactively investigating and addressing your child's worst habits while you're at home. Remove him from the situation as necessary. If you're out shopping and cannot handle the child's misbehavior, you may simply need to leave.

Correcting in public

If we are honest with ourselves, sometimes life simply doesn't allow us to not reprimand our children's mistakes in private. Think about the occasions your youngster has misbehaved in public. Sure, it's tough to bring attention to ourselves and the kid by punishing right then and there. But again, sometimes others evaluate us more if we don't modify our actions.

Many parents may tell themselves that they have the fortitude to stand up and leave if required, and they take pleasure in not correcting in public, but when push comes to shove, they may end up doing nothing at all. When it's blatantly evident that the youngster is misbehaving and upsetting others and you don't dare to leave, then, by all means, discipline him! It's more courteous to let them realize that you cherish their peace.

Printed in Great Britain
by Amazon